Learning from Jeff Bezos:
23 Principles

Karl Sipfle

Learning from Jeff Bezos: 23 Principles

© 2019 by Karl Sipfle. All rights reserved.

Learning from Jeff Bezos: 23 Principles

To Liz

Acknowledgements

With appreciation I would like to thank Dan Ammann and Mark Reuss, the former and current presidents of General Motors, for reading and listening to my ideas on a range of issues and encouraging their further development; to Bill Gates for his counsel years ago that stuck with me; and to Jeff Bezos for bringing humanity into space. These are leaders of planetary scale. I would like to thank my wife, Liz, for making the modern me possible. And, finally, I would like to thank you, the reader, for striving to achieve and improve, to the benefit of us all.

Figure 1: Space capsule in descent

Preface

Figure 2: Jeff and friends at the rocket factory

This book is a result of lectures I gave for VPs and Directors at General Motors, which proved very popular. Their enthusiastic feedback was encouraging, and I've fleshed out my chatter into what you now hold in your hands.

Spending actual time as a rocket scientist is exhilarating and challenging. Wherever you look, in transport of all kinds and well beyond, machines are changing- from merely computerized, to autonomous. At T minus 2 minutes, the computers take over a Blue Origin spaceship completely, and run the show until touchdown.

In addition to nominal operation, the ship monitors itself for any anomalies. If necessary, the space capsule itself rockets away from the big booster rocket. If the booster rocket becomes ill, it will deliberately fall out of the sky before passing over populated areas. All of this is done by computer. There is no pilot aboard the New Shepard.

This book includes both management and technical principles, with the fused theme being management of advanced technical programs. This book is also a view from inside, capturing how to actually do the remarkable and historic. All engineers and business people stand to benefit from its lessons. Principle 10 is to Teach Each Other. I am doing that now.

From Seattle, I was recruited by General Motors, drawn by autonomous cars, which are even more complicated. The training at GM features the concepts:

- Think for yourself. Don't blindly follow crowd movement, and
- Move. Resolutely and with commitment.

These statements could have come straight from the culture of Blue Origin!

Introduction

Figure 3: New Shepard booster gracefully lands

On November 23, 2015, for the first time in history, a rocket flew to space and then landed vertically. On January 22, 2016, this same rocket was refueled and reused in the same way. On April 2, 2016, this same rocket flew again, becoming the first to be *repeatedly* reused, and ushering in the era of routine, affordable spaceflight. For around $250,000, you will very soon be able to fly to space, an experience you will surely never forget, and the price will drop rapidly.

From that first landing to the rocket's eventual retirement to a museum, I had the pleasure of working in the spaceship factory of Jeff Bezos. This gave me the extraordinary opportunity to meet, study, and learn from the most successful entrepreneur and most ambitious entrepreneur who ever lived.

New Space

Figure 4: NASA slide

Three billionaires, masters of action, are at the front of commercial spaceflight

- ▶ Richard Branson (net worth $ 5 billion) - Virgin Galactic
- ▶ Elon Musk (net worth $ 20 billion)- SpaceX

  (Bill Gates (net worth $ 76 billion))
- ▶ Jeff Bezos (net worth $ 140 billion)- Blue Origin

SpaceX is in metro L.A., Virgin is near L.A., and Blue Origin is in Seattle, the HQ city of Amazon.

There are three key spaceflight steps that these men must achieve to realize their ultimate goals. There must be safety suitable for regular people. There must be economical reusability, as we have with airplanes. Finally, there must be orbital reach.

The three companies each have a different strategy and ordering for the key steps.

- ▶ Virgin   1. **Human** and **Re-Use** 2. **Orbit**?
- ▶ SpaceX   1. **Orbit** 2. **Re-Use** 3. **Human**
- ▶ Blue Origin   1. **Re-Use** 2. **Human** 3. **Orbit**

There is much that is new in the current era of spaceflight, so new that assumed engineering contexts have changed. For example, safety strategy must be reformulated, to serve days- or weeks-long space flights carrying many passengers. Passenger vehicles can autonomously launch and autonomously land. Advances in executable modeling, emergency reconfigurability, and simulation fidelity all serve the company mission. 3-D printing allows advanced manufacturing that was completely impractical just a few years ago.

Meet Jeff Bezos

Figure 5: Jeff as a child

"Hi, I'm Jeff," said the smiling man before me in jeans and boots, as we stood beside a glass wall overlooking a rocket factory. With a handshake, my journey was under way in earnest, joining this man's project to create from scratch one of the biggest steps in humanity's development and future history.

Jeff Bezos, like Steve Jobs, and Dave Thomas of Wendy's, was a young adoptee. As though an omen, he was raised in Houston.

He is a computer science grad from Princeton, who worked on Wall Street before founding Amazon, one of the first companies on the Internet, in 1994.

Six years later, in 2000, he founded Blue Origin (2 years before SpaceX and 4 years before Virgin Galactic). It has been said that Amazon was simply a vehicle to make money to fund his space company, a rumor he says he "can neither confirm nor deny."

Jeff bought and expanded the family ranch in west Texas, where he spent summers as a youth, and where he has built his launch pad for New Shepard flights (New Glenn will be built and launched at Cape Canaveral).

Thanks mostly to Amazon, he is 15% of the way to *trillionaire*, where no man has gone before.

National Merit Scholar, Valedictorian, Phi Betta Kappa, and now the richest man in the world, he reigns as dean of space transport for the people.

Figure 6: Jeff as a teen

Meet Amazon

Figure 7: Amazon HQ, Seattle

Everyone knows the public Amazon. Before settling into chosen positions over a long career, I've interviewed with Google, SpaceX, and so on, and several groups inside Amazon, which was telling.

In my opinion the real secret to the mega-success of an Amazon is to take a plain concept- retail- currently running with regular people doing the usual things, and vigorously apply high intelligence, creativity, and intensity to dominate profoundly. Tremendous lengths are taken at Amazon to apply technology and attitude to delight the customer and to get better and better.

If you go, too, the first person you meet will be a manager, or people person of some kind. You will notice immediately a conspicuous brightness and energy. This continues unabated throughout the long day. Of each clever candidate, this manager will ask, "if Amazon were your company, what product or business would you add?" Then he or she writes it down.

Rendered to a room encrusted with whiteboards, one individual or team after another will present you with expected and unexpected problems. They want to know how you think. All software-based companies want to know how you think, but the person across *this* desk is sharper.

As you answer, the questions will become more elaborate. What if this happens, how would you handle that, how would you scale what you have presented to national coverage, how does this actually work at a low level? One guy just walked in, placed a Rubik's cube on the desk, and said, "write me code to solve this," and sat quietly and watched.

Jeff accumulated people like this for six years before starting his space company. He had a trove to draw from, which he did.

Meet Seattle

Figure 8: Seattle skyline

Sitting in the Seattle airport wearing a Blue Origin sweater, I'm approached by a man who worked at Blue Origin in its earliest days. Today he runs laboratories for Charles Simonyi- billionaire, early employee of Microsoft, and the first tourist to fly to space twice.

Seattle is the center of the Universe for the *top* entrepreneur. Companies who do not start there (SpaceX, Cruise) show up in search of talent. My apartment (with rent equal to my Midwest McMansion mortgage payment) lay within ten miles of the homes of both Gates and Bezos, and Liz and I frequented their favored restaurants and met the family friends. Amazon's facilities sit on land owned by the late Paul Allen, another Microsoft billionaire and Seattle resident and founder of major research labs.

While San Francisco excels in creating wealth often out of vapor and money-losing companies, all the billionaires in Seattle, home of Starbucks, too, actually delivered product to millions of people before getting mega-rich.

Seattle is beyond can-do or get-rich-quick or change-the-world-with-a-phone-app. Seattle looks to the sky. Transformative, actual change on a planetary scale is the order of the day.

All of this is in, not a San Francisco or New York, but a metro area that does not make the top 100 in the world by population. It is concentrated intellect, wealth, and power. And it is lovely and temperate.

Where a local bar might be frequented by car guys and gals in metro Detroit, in Seattle it's plane and rocket engineers and technicians, and the "mom and pop" companies are aerospace shops. And software. Lots and lots of software.

Meet Blue Origin

Figure 9: New Shepard first successful landing

Rob Myerson, president of Blue Origin at the time, is a fellow U Michigan grad who shares and even surpasses my own high interest in space. Blue Origin at Mission 2 was about 400 people, mostly engineers (rocket scientists). The staff is made of people from NASA, the Space Shuttle program (including astronauts), missile programs, and standard and new space companies such as Boeing and Aerojet Rocketdyne and Bigelow and Virgin. The software people include many who jumped off the Amazon and Microsoft treadmills.

The Boeing guys were well aware of how wet behind the ears some of the "kids" were, but polite, and just kept quiet at certain times. The paradoxical contrast between the two huge Seattle industries, the sober and majestic aerospace business and the more seat-of-the-pants software engineers, is a defining characteristic of the local industry and culture.

The Christmas parties featured fun and goofy skits of a mock Star Trek episode, the chief program manager as an opera singer, and puppet representations of the two emblematic tortoises- the ambling Gradatim and the hyper Ferociter. As Blue became increasingly successful and attracted a lot of attention (from the

US Space Command, and United Launch Alliance, for example), the partying became more staid and the silliness was banished (but, fortunately, retained in the video archives).

Bottles of fine whisky adorn the tops of people's cabinets, and a week of exertion sometimes would be concluded in such a way with teammates without leaving the premises.

In addition to the control room in Texas was a sister one at HQ. Sometimes for a launch Jeff would go to Texas, sometimes he would be in the front row at HQ watching the monitors. But always, he wears his lucky boots.

Jeff maintains a controlling interest in his wealth machine, Amazon, and complete ownership of Blue. He enjoys complete, independent power to execute his decisions without delay.

As is typical for a domestic aerospace company, a very large American flag adorns the wall of the manufacturing building. The work is a source of deep pride for all the participants, and it is cutting edge.

Easy to miss the importance of, until you tour the plant, is that Blue Origin is not just *constructing* spaceships, it is *manufacturing* them. These craft are part of the ongoing mission to get humanity into space *en masse.*

Figure 10: "We are of Blue Origin."

Blue Origin Vision and Programs

Figure 11: Future Tourism

The Vision of Blue Origin can be described thus:

- ▶ Our Vision is millions of people living and working in space.
- ▶ We Will Build the Infrastructure for Space Transport, Making Possible the Works of the Next Generation of Entrepreneurs, as happened before with the Internet.
- ▶ Heavy industry can be moved to space and Earth can be a garden, zoned residential and light industrial.
- ▶ Until this process is well under way, space will suck because there is no bacon and no whisky there.

There were several early programs at Blue Origin used to develop the knowledge to get to a working New Shephard. These were for the Charon, PM-1 (Propulsion Module 1), and PM-2 vehicles, all of which flew to some extent.

There are two programs active today. The *New Shepard* program, named after the first American in space, is the suborbital rocket designed for experimental payloads and, especially, space tourism. In addition to continuing to increase knowledge about the vehicle and its refinement, ongoing tourism will provide some revenue to reduce or complement the $1 billion per year personal outlay from Jeff (obtained by cashing in Amazon stock).

The complete New Shepard vehicle consists of the booster rocket (the PM-4), which touches down upright on its four legs, and the space capsule (the CC-2), which features six huge windows next to six reclined seats, and lands by parachute.

Very far along is also the *New Glenn* program, named after the first American in orbit. Along with a large space capsule, it features a rocket far larger than New Shepard's (but sharing some of the technology). The rocket is so large that it is being built near the launch pad in Cape Canaveral, on its side in a new building created for that purpose.

A New Glenn mission to the moon is sometimes called the *New Armstrong* program (so far, there is no *New Kirk* program).

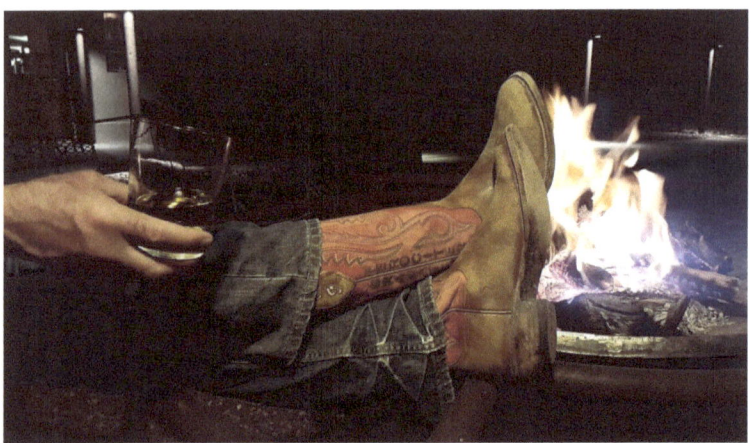

Figure 12: Jeff after another successful launch

PRINCIPLES

Learning from Jeff Bezos: 23 Principles

1. Gradatim Ferociter

Figure 13: Blue Origin emblem

With every periodic chunk of time, despite the hardships and setbacks and original targets, try to always get closer to the end goal, and just keep pushing forward.

When you come to Blue Origin for an interview, you first notice two things. The first is that the HQ building is unmarked. But once you get past the gate and across the entry lot, emblazoned across the front steps in foot-tall, inlaid, brass letters is the motto, greeting, and battle cry "Gradatim Ferociter." This is Latin for "step by step, ferociously." A company email will often end with this phrase.

Human spaceflight is an extremely challenging endeavor. The first major step has been accomplished by powerful governments with hyper-enormous amounts of money. Re-use that is actually cheaper than the very expensive build-and-expend, was not achieved by them.

Spacecraft that can fly over and over like other forms of transport, economically, and safe enough for regular people, is an engineering feat requiring the best teams on Earth. In so doing, most aspects of the original problem, from structural dynamics to computerization to manufacturing to safety, must be revisited and thought about anew.

What this requires, in addition to genius, is persistence in great quantities.

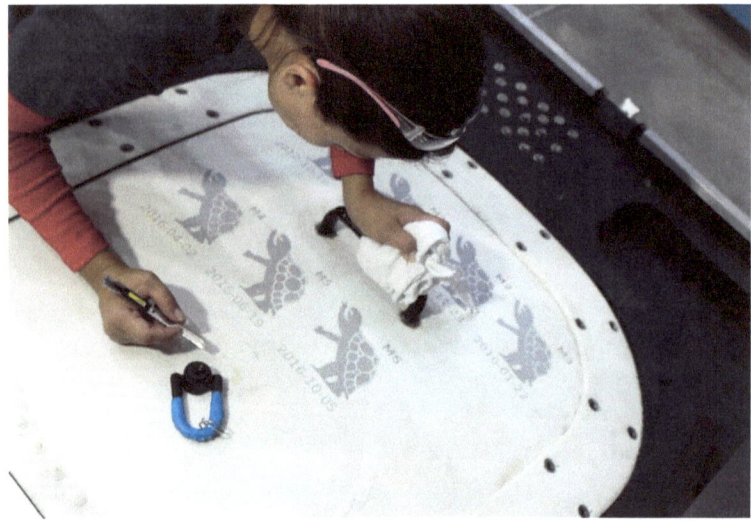

Figure 14: Another successful mission, another tortoise

2. Safety Vigilance

Figure 15: Former Space Shuttle Commander and early Head of Safety, Jeff Ashby

- ▶ The first document that a new employee reads after the welcome letter from Jeff is the Mission Assurance Plan.
- ▶ All engineers are expected to bring any concerns directly to the Director of Safety.
- ▶ All engineers are trained on safety engineering.

- ▶ No forms and no process required for the reporter, no focus on liability.
- ▶ Mind-to-mind dialog, efficient, complete, and accurate.
- ▶ Large System Engineers group designs.
- ▶ Small Safety group evaluates.
- ▶ Failover design defined early by System Engineers.

This way of being requires both transparency and involvement. Safety is not a task just for "the Safety people," and certainly not for the lawyers.

In addition, it requires a fresh look and creative response. This is because the context has changed; spaceflight is to be used differently than before, and that affects the realities for safety.

For example, for the first time, ordinary people will soon be lofted by the dozens into quiescent orbits for days or weeks at a time aboard a computer-piloted vessel.

Until now, missions of planes and spacecraft have been either of far shorter duration, or been enormous, expensive government projects to achieve the barely-working to be piloted by professional risk-takers. These vessels all spend a lot of their time, especially substantial-risk time, working their systems, rather than coasting. A key safety principle in aerospace has been to keep things as simple *and fixed*- unchangeable after takeoff- as possible. The thinking is that trying to add a basket of system features to respond to anomalies actually increases the chance of some malfunction in the whole resulting system, while there will be little opportunity to work effectively to fix a serious problem should one arise.

In the new, orbital scenario we have the possibility of something bad happening in a large vessel in day 2 of a 20-day mission, the result, if not addressed, being the eventual, certain death of a score of people. In this case, the purposely-created situation of not being able to change anything is not acceptable. The strategy must change because the context in which the conventional policies were developed has changed (this was a personal contribution of mine to Blue Origin, in which I take pride because it may save lives). From the new strategy come specific changes in architecture, development, and operations.

3. Hire Very Smart, Knowledgeable Adults and Trust Them to Make Good Decisions

Figure 16: image: blueorigin.com

▶ 3-page Employee Manual

In one swoop this simple and important principle mostly eliminates the ubiquitous twin threats for an intense, go-go tech company of inadequate skill and personal career treachery. While both were in evidence in pockets, in large measure the theoretical ideal was realized in practice.

An example of this principle at work is Brandon Haber, the current Director of Software for New Shepard. He is a Computer Science grad with 4 years of experience at United Space Alliance, a year plus at Bigelow Aerospace, and 4 years in Seattle writing avionics software, before coming to Blue.

People from Stanford, MIT, and NASA are everywhere; they are your team members. Among the stellar individuals I met there was the safety leader, Andrew. The duds are few.

Orientation at Blue included a boast that the employee policy manual was only three pages long and basically just said "don't do anything stupid."

4. Hire People who Already Have a Passion for the Company's Mission

Figure 17: image: blueoriigin.com

Making advanced spaceships is really hard. You need people who are not only extraordinarily able, but passionate and determined and persistent. You also need real Systems Engineering, which eschews hacking and requires discipline.

Blue Origin is able to give many people their dream job, which is an enormous strength for a company to have. People will work longer hours for less money, and with far more desire that it be done superbly.

To be hired by Blue Origin requires five things. First is the usual resume. With it, is expected an essay on why you have a personal need to do this kind of work. This essay is passed around with the resume and is a serious part of the hiring decision. The third element is the usual detailed questioning by several people, probing the quality of your mind and, secondarily, your knowledge. And, fifth, is a Powerpoint presentation, to a large conference room full of your prospective peers and bosses, about yourself and why the richest man on Earth should hire you for his favorite project.

5. Treat Your People Well and Make Things Easy- They Are Busy and Working Hard on Hard Problems

Figure 18: Posing with Buzz Aldrin and New Shepard

- ▶ Quiet park on the grounds
- ▶ Catered meal every week
- ▶ Free drinks and snacks
- ▶ No hassles getting reimbursed
- ▶ Workplace that is homey
- ▶ Full kitchen
- ▶ Dogs welcome

It is a strange experience, the first time, of having one's deep, technical thoughts broken apart by a sudden loud spat between one's coworkers' dogs.

Blue Origin offices are a home, and that is no accident; the building renovation was put in that direction by Jeff. The environment is visually comfortable and outfitted with conveniences to keep you as undistracted as you would like from your rocket thoughts. The kitchen is central, available to all, and continuously stocked with as many snacks and drinks as you could want. It is possible to come hungry in the morning and leave at midnight, with all needs adequately met.

A private garden adjoining the building has been built for strolling, having a get-together, or feeding the fish.

The very best hors d'oeuvres I've ever experienced are at the Christmas party.

As with other first class, smart companies, there is no hassle getting reimbursed for expenses.

6. "You Are the People That Figure Out Problems That Have Never Been Solved"

Figure 19: image: blueorigin.com

▶ We Do Not Just Know What is Known, We Make New Knowledge.

▶ Don't just do what everyone else does without thinking about the problem.

▶ Do Not Believe Others Who Say It Is Too Difficult to Solve!

Blue Origin is not a place for people who are just scholars. A scholar is someone who knows everything there is to know about what *other* people think. Blue Origin already contains

knowledge. They care how, and how well, *you* think. (In fact, many there are not old enough to be scholars.)

If you visit Amazon in Seattle, you will find the same attitude. While this is en vogue for computer people, the Bezos companies take it up a notch (or two).

Everywhere the HQ building is filled with inspiration. In the foyer, the ten-foot tall rotating model of Earth has been replaced by wall-sized pictures above Earth taken by their spaceship. If you are an employee you can proceed straight through a door to the private gym, but otherwise you climb the stairs where you will end up in front of a full-scale, extremely detailed replica of the spaceship in Jules Verne's *From the Earth to the Moon;* small meetings are held inside. A few feet from there you will find my first desk, hanging above which is the actual model of the Jupiter-bound spaceship from the movie 2001: A Space Odyssey (the home of HAL, the intelligent computer).

On the way you will pass more, genuine space artifacts, such as engines and spacesuits, and the actual models of the Enterprise and space dock from the movies, all in glass cases. Jeff played a Starfleet official in the film *Star Trek Beyond*.

Everywhere on the walls are painted quotations, from Leonardo, Shaw, and one from a favorite author of mine, Antoine de Saint-Exupery. All of these speak to the topic, as Goethe puts it, that "boldness has beauty, power, and magic in it."

It took me weeks or months of passing a long drawing encased on a certain wall before I noticed it was the original stem-to-stern engineering drawing of the Saturn rocket. A sense of history being made is everywhere. Another famous drawing lays out in detail the expected progress of human expansion into space over the next centuries.

7. Good Ideas Can Come from Any Team Member

Figure 20: The BE-4 orbital engine

▶ Extreme listening to everyone for ideas, and reliance upon them.

▶ Even interns are placed on important work.

Blue Origin is extremely serious about this point, which comes from Jeff himself, who is known for listening to and conversing with anyone in the room. People right out of college can make 1-on-1 presentations to him. For launches, he is embedded with the rest of the staff and it is a mutual (and supremely exciting) experience.

8. Personal Experience Matters

Figure 21: The landed booster

▶ Jeff "doesn't have time to wait for some people to acquire experience"

For all the emphasis on originality and on fresh thinking, there are needs to foresee, in certain roles, that can only adequately come from experience. Jeff's extreme bias toward fresh thinking, unsurprisingly, is tempered by realism.

9. Learn from Humanity's Past

Figure 22: Neil Armstrong

- ▶ Studied the failure of the Challenger disaster
  - ▶ Management caved.
  - ▶ Normalization of deviation.
- ▶ Studied the Success of the Apollo Program

▶ Culture Matters.

Smart people think. Really smart people think about thinking. The failure of the Challenger disaster and the incredible success of the US moon shot have both been extensively studied. The conclusions provide insight as to how a space organization should behave and carry itself to succeed.

What was found in the Disaster is that leadership caved in their decision under pressure, and that the engineers became accustomed to singed O-rings as normal.

Similarly, a key finding on what made the big difference in the moon-shot case, was that it was a cultural attitude of personal humility and gratitude rather than power struggles or self-aggrandizement. The latter not only ruffle feathers on the team, but also distort critical judgement.

The winning values have been purposely weaved into the Blue Origin expectations, starting from the first day of orientation.

10. Teach Each Other

Figure 23: Blue Origin craft

▶ After a difficult problem is solved, a presentation is made to the whole company as to how it was done.

▶ Supports knowing the whole machine.

During these lectures, Jeff was often there listening and asking questions- good, engineering questions.

Besides the immediate value in broadening and stretching the engineers and sharing ideas, the continuing practice leads toward everyone knowing everything about the machine, how it is supposed to work, and therefor what interactions between parts can go wrong. This importantly enhances safety. In this practice, I can confirm that Blue Origin is way ahead of other companies.

11. The Joy of Not Doing Things

Figure 24: The landed space capsule on the desert floor

▶ Eliminate unnecessary process.

▶ Do not eliminate necessary process.

In a typical company, time and opportunity get wasted doing things that "have" to be done, that have very little to do with the company's goals, safety, law, or ethics. Oftentimes, the fruit includes increased complexity as well. These things are brought in from the dark side of collaboration and experience and driven by groupthink and social negotiation to maintain harmony and secure position. In order to avoid (reduce) these problems, the company needs to explicitly state and live in opposition to them.

While a complete abhorrence of process would be very naïve, a superior solution to heavy process intended to avoid dumb mistakes, is to require a very smart staff. This is a fundamental, and often tacit, West Coast assumption, and the success thereby generated cannot be argued with.

In practice this economy of method usually leads to a measure of cliquishness, as some arbitrary micro-rules will develop organically to fill the vacuum, to the benefit of some individuals and detriment of others. Experienced managers know this. The company and the mission benefit overall, and the personal dedication that is expected overcomes much of the friction. (It then becomes a company decision, made purposely or by default, whether to encourage or discourage the stronger peer personalities being the source of these rules.)

12. Accept Mistakes as Inevitable When Doing Great and Difficult Things

Figure 25: Jeff Bezos

▶ High Tolerance for Failure

▶ Employee blew up a half-million-dollar prototype plus test stand without being disciplined or dismissed

This long-standing Bezos principle bears on today's "fail fast" philosophy. A difference in the details, though, is that Jeff expects that you have well thought things out in advance, and not plunged in too fast.

13. People Need to be There

Figure 26: image: blueorigin.com

Before New Shepard, a series of sub-space test craft were built and flown. The first to fly to high altitudes was the rocket immediately preceding New Shepard, the PM-2. This craft was lost on its maiden high-altitude flight, gyrating violently until it disintegrated.

Though much safer overall than automobiles, every time there is any crash in the aerospace business there is an in-depth investigation. The chief finding for the PM-2 was that a key engineer, who had been allowed by his manager to work remotely, would have caught the problem in the development process had he been embedded in the team like the others. The engineer and the manager were both found to be at fault and a policy against such remote work was instituted.

Learning from Jeff Bezos: 23 Principles

14. Accentuate What Went Right

Figure 27: Overview of work

This principle nicely complements principle #1- Gradatim Ferociter.

Several months before I started at Blue Origin was New Shepard Mission 1, using serial number 1 of this new rocket design. My buddies at Blue told me what the day was like.

Mission 1 achieved all of the mission profile in as far as had all of humanity's previous flights of a parachute-landing space capsule atop a booster rocket. The ascent was good, and the capsule landed as intended, ready for the next flight it would take. The chief innovation, however- that the booster rocket engine would relight after a free fall and land the booster gently-

failed to materialize, converting the gleaming vehicle a hundred man-years in the making into wreckage on the desert floor.

Upon this happening, the primary dream-holder behind the project left the control room for a few minutes. On Jeff's return, before the sullen team, he grabbed a marker and began listing on a whiteboard all the things that had gone right. After all, this craft had never flown before. Everything preceding had been a ground test or a simulation. System after system had worked as intended on first flight.

Inspired by this leadership, the exhausted crew returned to the Big Mission. A second booster was built. Remarkably for a new rocket business, there has been a 100 per cent success rate in the list of missions since.

15. Lean Management

Figure 28: PM-4 reclining at home

▶ Only 3 people were between the engineer and Jeff Bezos.

This principle, too, was boasted about during orientation. On my arrival there were only three layers of management- president, director, manager- between the troops and Jeff.

Directors led regular gatherings of their whole departments, at which everyone spoke up. The president was very present, knew and greeted the first 500 people by name, and led the monthly company-wide meetings. Most important of all, of course, is that he is a fellow alumnus of the University of Michigan; sporting a U-M t-shirt would win a smile.

It was at the monthly meetings that each and every new recruit was introduced to the whole company. The intended team spirit manifested quite well, aided by the company's singular and lofty mission.

16. All Areas Must Have a Leader, and The Leader Must Decide

Figure 29: A tour for the VP

▶ Sole decision responsibility and authority

Despite a very (very) egalitarian attitude toward idea creation and exploitation, there was no utopian confusion clouding the seriousness of the decisions to be made and their consequences. This was further enhanced by the presence of some staff with a military background. And the studied cases of the past such as Challenger and the Moon Shot, made clear the need for clear responsibility and excellence in judgement.

It was stressed that leaders were carefully chosen for their judgement, and that they carried full responsibility for their departments' decisions, and therefore full authority to make them. If need be, a unanimous recommendation by his or her staff was expected to be overridden by a manager who believed differently. This recapturing of the obvious protects passengers from trendy but ill-advised management style alternatives.

17. If Anything is Blocking Your Progress, Notify at Once

Figure 30: Lift-off

▶ Wednesday Process Exception meetings with Jeff

▶ Requests and Their Fates Published as Examples

There is great emphasis at Blue on making sure forward motion is speedy and smart. A certain amount of process was expected to be necessary. But it was not only allowed but much-encouraged that a party could "sue" for exemption from normal process in the interest of speed, making his case directly to the judge, who was Jeff. Jeff would devote an afternoon a week for availability for just this purpose. If no one showed up, he would email the whole company saying that he was sitting on his hands in the cafeteria, lonely and with nothing to do.

If you needed a machine costing millions of dollars ASAP, you made your case. Some decisions were immediate. If there was subtlety to the matter, you would be asked to write a six-page memo and come back. Successful proposals were then published as examples.

Skipping process was not reckless, however. Recall that Principle #1 is *Step-by-step*, ferociously. My one inquiry to Jeff in this area was as to whether he would also be interested in places where there might be too *little* process. His one-word response was "Yes."

At today's electrified, self-driving auto company we learn how to "Go Slow to Go Fast" in very large-scale projects. At Blue it is put "Slow is smooth and smooth is fast." In other words, Gradatim Ferociter.

18. Conservative Implementations of Advanced Architectures

Figure 31: View downward from the separated capsule

Jeff's approach is to seek strong architectures: designs that are robust, simple, and powerful, that can be used as intellectual and engineering backbone for years to come. That makes possible implementations that are well within the limits and tolerant of minor faults. It allows for an ever refined and tested approach that becomes ever safer and better understood with the progression of time.

This is the Principle I printed out and hung over my desk as daily direction.

19. The Machine Should be Simple and Well-Understood

Figure 32: BE-4, the orbital engine

- ▶ This is what Safety and Reliability organically flow from.
- ▶ This Principle is highlighted in the Mission Assurance Plan.

This can be applied to any "machine," for example, an organization of first responders. At Blue Origin, the emphasis is on space vehicles. It means the organism will perform reliably and as designed.

It also refers to Principle #2: Safety Vigilance. Well-Understood by Whom? The answer is: the entire engineering staff. It is critical that the chief architects are clear-minded in what they lay down; the entire corpus of the engineering staff thereafter become tripwires catching errors in thinking and implementation, which ultimately go to Safety.

20. Agile *Development,* but Pre-Defined *Design*

Figure 33: New Glenn

- ▶ Basis for Approval of Safety-Critical Software document
- ▶ Basis for Approval of Safety-Critical Hardware document
- ▶ In-House Software Development Plan
- ▶ Architecture Design Description document
- ▶ Hardware Architecture Design Description document
- ▶ Software Architecture Design Description document

▶ Draw from DO-178 and ISO 26262

▶ Architecture documents are not a retrospective of emergent design

▶ High-level requirements are peer-reviewed before low-level design is executed

In the engineering world at large, two big revolutions occurred, originally in software engineering and then widely deployed, inspired by the crisis of the over-cost and over-schedule software debacles of the 60's and 70's. First was the formalization of the software development process, which secured a moderately successful grip on the crisis but also brought development speed to a crawl. A reaction to this the was the family of "Agile" methodologies, flourishing in the go-go era of the Web and games and mobile phone apps and adopted by big software companies.

Where the world is struggling to find truth, is in where exactly the truth lies between these two polar camps, and what is typically missed, is that the answer is based on what the real question is. Agile is the right business answer to survival and boom of a product, such as those fuel-able by Silicon valley megabucks, where frequent "crashes" are only in the figurative sense, the consequences of such are mild, lateness to market is death, and it is not known for sure what precisely is the product the customer will be satisfied with and buy, despite what they say at the outset.

A company like Blue Origin does not have a wavering, varying product goal; its focus is laser-sharp. It has little need to please investor communities or exchanges as it is privately funded for a committed purpose. And the product "exploding" is tremendously costly in both human and business terms. This is no place for "coding and design happening at the same time," which is the definition of true Agile.

The smartest solution is to exploit the true rapidity, and capture the fine minds that work this way, during the detailed development phase- where most of the time should be spent- under the constraints of a solid architecture specification that anticipates the *system-wide* interactions and implementations, which scientific study has shown to be the birthplace of the nastiest problems. Thus-protected and freed for the most part from these concerns, the "stallions" can race heads-down to their goals.

A full flowering and refinement of this basic method the author describes as "DEFT." Contact him for further details.

21. First-Level Decisions First

Figure 34: Passenger capsule

▶ Do not waste time discussing, or be influenced by, detail that does not matter until higher-level decisions are made. Focus on those higher decisions first.

This is top-down organized design *of thought*. This is what computer scientists schooled in Jeff's (and my) era naturally do. Creative flights of thought are good things worth exploiting, but disorderly thought in charge is a Really Bad Idea in the spaceship business.

22. Data-Driven

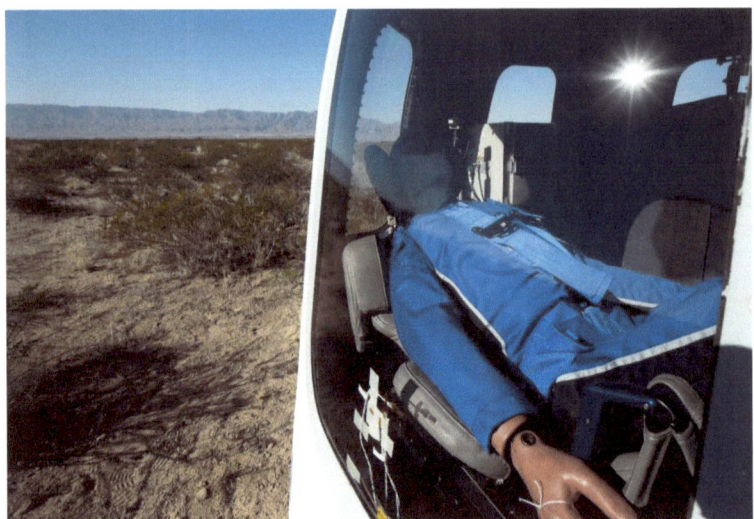

Figure 35: Mannequin Skywalker has landed

▶ Decisions should be Data-Driven.

This very simple, strong, and popular principle was embraced early by Jeff Bezos and Amazon. It serves even better today, with so many fierce and diverse opinions often traceable to personal agendas, desires, and wishes.

This principle also means that in the face of new and better data or realization of better thinking, one must be willing to change one's mind, and publicly. The best thinkers and leaders have the confidence to do this.

23. Most Important Decisions to be Made Can Be Sufficiently Discussed in Six Pages

Figure 36: Jeff Bezos

▶ Often requested by Jeff.

▶ Rapid decision-making even over millions of dollars.

▶ Well-informed decisions.

In Jeff's view, decisions to be made of all types- administrative or technical- are best discussed in memos of six pages. The number appears to be a product of experience.

This very simple and memorable directive makes it easy for the less-experienced to grasp what degree of detail is good in making one's case, and tells everyone what Jeff is looking for, which saves time.

Learning from Jeff Bezos: 23 Principles

Figure 37: blueorigin.com

Spaceflight Terms

Autonomous

Flying under its own control, using on-board computers.

FRR

Flight Readiness Review, the final team review to clear the craft for lift-off

Automatic Sequence Start

The point, near the end of the countdown, when manual control is relinquished, and operation of the craft is handed to the computers.

Max q

The point of maximum mechanical stress (dynamic pressure) on the vehicle during its ascent, while it accelerates against the air.

MECO

Main Engine Cut-Off. The point at which engines are turned off and the craft coasts from its accumulated speed.

Touchdown

Successful landing.

About the Author

Karl Sipfle is a Senior Lead Architect for GM's autonomous electric vehicles. He is an alumnus of Blue Origin in Avionics Software. While at Blue Origin he devised new safety engineering theory.

With 45 years of software, electronics, and management experience extending from the West Coast to Wall Street to Europe to South America, Karl has worked on autonomous land, air, and space vehicles starting in 2000, and simulators since 2009.

Karl is a computer science grad from the University of Michigan in Ann Arbor, from whence the entire crew of Apollo 15 received degrees. He is a former voting officer of the Triple Nine Society.

www.ingramcontent.com/pod-product-compliance
Lightning Source LLC
Chambersburg PA
CBHW041942240526
45473CB00033B/208